AUTOBIOGRAPHY OF A MARGUERITE

Also by Zarah Butcher-McGunnigle

Nostalgia Has Ruined My Life
Leaves Fall Off to Create Drama

ZARAH BUTCHER-McGUNNIGLE

AUTOBIOGRAPHY OF A MARGUERITE

First published in 2014
by Hue & Cry Press
This edition first published in 2026
from the Writing and Society Research Centre
at Western Sydney University
by the Giramondo Publishing Company
PO Box 557
Willoughby NSW 2068 Australia
www.giramondopublishing.com

Cover design by Allison Colpoys
Series design by Jenny Grigg
Typesetting by Andrew Davies
in 9/15 pt Tiempos Regular

Photographs courtesy Zarah Butcher-Mcgunnigle

Printed and bound by Pegasus Media & Logistics
Distributed in Australia by NewSouth Books

A catalogue record for this book is available from the
National Library of Australia.

ISBN: 978-1-923106-61-1

9 8 7 6 5 4 3 2 1

The Giramondo Publishing Company acknowledges the support of Western Sydney
University in the implementation of its book publishing program.

This project has been assisted by the Commonwealth Government through Creative
Australia, its arts funding and advisory body.

For my mother, Marguerite

Love your disease: it's keeping you healthy
Dr John Harrison

I am writing a story about a girl who is not me.
I cannot prove she is not me.
Janet Frame, from 'Jan Godfrey'

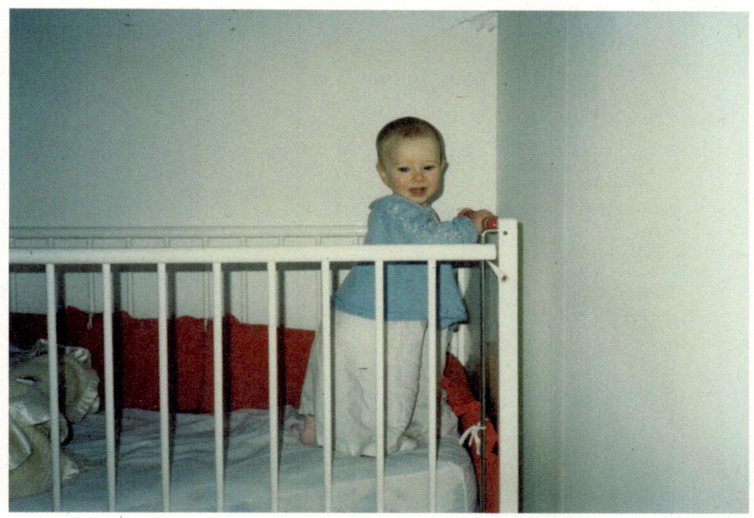

It is not even a story. Every day I have to cross a bridge. The patient back and forth motion. The patient back and forth. The patient's back. The patience. Everything you've done so far you've done to care for yourself. Is this what you want to convey. 'Pain is not interesting,' but it is. I could get money for this but I don't. The disadvantages must be set against the advantages. Do you want me to be practical or honest.

My mother stands in the garden. She says, I can't hear you. She says, is this a weed or not. The phone rings and it's for my mother, but she won't come inside, so I stand in for her. Is this a weed or not, she says, holding up the blistered plant.

We package ourselves to the doctor. I have symptoms, and what's more, I have signs. What are your symptoms, the doctor asks me. Her symptoms are X, Y, Z, my mother answers.

(during the early afternoon) She was in the garden, inventing a harvest (corn, wheat), flooding, shaking, radius. (My sister needs glasses, my sister gets headaches, seizures.) Frowning camera. Jumping from the tree, self-timer. (Therefore I want glasses, seizures.) I get stomach pains if I am around people too long (a few hours). Hopeless natural waste kernel. Aggressive bird. What kind of pains do you get? Oak tree pains. (When I was a girl, I jumped from the oak tree repeatedly, trying to break a leg.)

A location in the waiting room but no extent. My mother has taken time off work, or maybe she has quit work. I am given a questionnaire, we complete it. I print my name very slowly. You'll have to go quicker than that, my mother says. There's a magazine in her lap, she's not reading it, she's reading over my shoulder. Question: How would you describe the pain? For example, is it like being stabbed with a piece of glass. My mother takes the paper from me, Would it be helpful if I did the writing. But I don't know, I say, I've never been stabbed with a piece of glass.

Ached, pillaging, dampen. Lollygag. (But mother. You bought her an ice cream the last time she went to the doctor.) Nothing rhymes with orange, but I like orange-flavoured confectionery. Confect, infect. Regarding pain, regarding value. (Yes but she was really sick, her headache was very bad.)

I stop going to school. All the days feel the same, I am held on a needle until another loop passes through me, waiting to be a product, something of value. For we were saved in this hope, but hope that is seen is not hope. I need something else, so my grandmother tries to teach me to knit. One narrative theory is that one never dies in knitting. Are you watching me, she says. Outside there is no weather. But my watch has stopped, I say.

We were going to. After switching damaging recovery. (we need more pronouns.) Grass aches against the epicentre of baldness. Since, may, continuous, concede. (Mother. Move your hair. The bald spot is showing.) To abnormalise: (Describe the worst event in your childhood). To thaw pre-frozen emotion: (Imagine you've just won a prize. What do your parents say).

On a floured surface, pressed and stretched with the back of the hand, folded over, rotated repeatedly. I cannot stand in one place for very long, because of my knees. The cookbook on the bench is called *I Hate to Cook*. My mother comes into the kitchen and says, I need the oven soon, so hurry up. My friend B calls me on the phone when my hands are covered in dough. I don't want to speak but I do. There's no need to worry, he says, which means, there's no need for him to worry, there's no need for him to worry about me, or to worry about my worrying. I look at my knees and they are like dough. The knee joint connects to the thigh and consists of two articulations, one between the femur and tibia, and one between the femur and patella. I'm not articulate. What am I trying to prove. My mother comes into the kitchen and says, I need you.

I can *see* you don't believe me. (Take off the lid.) Supplementary to the rest of. The whole would be unchanged if. I can't *see* your point. (when I walked in the street, I didn't look at people's faces because I didn't want them to look at my face. Why are you looking at me.) Ectropionised: rhymes with: disguised, criticised, patronised, generalised, traumatised, hospitalised, pressurised, unorganised, parenthesised.

God won't help me, so I have to read self-help books. I have time on my hands. I have to stay inside. I am watching everything very closely: myself, the pine trees, the pot plants, the rain, the furniture. I can see myself from the perspective of myself and I can also see myself from the perspective of the pine trees, the pot plants, the rain, the furniture. What I mean to say is. I am inside and outside at the same time. I have time on my hands. I have to stay at home. I have to hurry up and read the books before they are due back at the library. Last night I dreamt that I blew my nose and something like a placenta came out. I open a self-help book that is about reading self-help books. The preface says, If you are reading this, you are beyond self-help. I think about myself as a child, I see my face and it doesn't seem real. The uterus of the forest, the wind blowing through it, under the pine needles. I think about myself lying on a bed, covered in needles. I am going to an acupuncturist once a week. Not because I want my symptoms reduced, but because I want to be touched.

What we choose to digest. She was fed by her. Heavy, severe, arduous, pouring, bodyguard. Heavy (You must eat or you'll be weak). Baked, sugared, fried, mostly, vastly, brightly, generally. My mother, broken sun inside the teacup. Drink it before it gets cold. (No one else was eating the cake, I felt bad that it might go to waste, I felt responsible, I had another piece, another, another piece.) I'm always crashing into the future.

I cough onto the window. Outside the window the street is eating itself. I am eating a piece of bread, chewing as if I can't decide whether to swallow. I need to go outside but my neighbour is out there. I'm waiting until she goes away.

She goes away and I go outside. But I was wrong, she didn't go away, she was still there, but I couldn't see her, she had gone into her garage momentarily. My neighbour is wearing complementary colours which hurt my eyes. She is holding a pair of hedge clippers. She says hello. I say hello back, but not in the tone that one usually says hello, more in the tone that one would say *sandwich*. I don't look her in the eye. She asks me where I am going. I am going to the hospital, I say. It's the third time I've broken my arm this year. She bends down to cut the head off a dandelion. Is that so, she says. Well, did you know, once I went to three weddings in a month.

Gut weather, needled weekend, needed a forecast, a qualifier. (I suppose I shouldn't complain. Think about people who are _____.) (How was your weekend?) Congested, squeezed, chalked, coped. Weak end of. (I didn't do anything) Tract (Who in your family was 'always sick'?) On a scale of, Expected, tracked, weakened, trapped. To detract: (The world is difficult. I want someone to look after me).

Last time I was here I filled in a form, or maybe I filled it out. I hate forms. After last time, I formed an opinion. I cannot articulate the opinion, but I know I formed one. On a scale of one to ten, I can never just pick one number. On a scale of one to then. The doctor is looking at my form. I nod and smile when she says something I don't hear. On the desk is a packet of 'non-sterile' latex gloves. She leans closer to me, pointing at the form. So, when rating your progress, from the choices of: quicker than expected, as expected, and slower than expected, you circled *my progress is slower than I expected*. Why did you circle that?

I don't know. Because I'm still in pain, because I noticed improvement before and now I don't? I look at my watch, but I'm not wearing a watch. The doctor says, Sure, but, is progress slower than you expected or slower than you hoped?

repeatedly, sweating inference, unable to concentrate, unable to sleep. Generalisation: (what's the use?). Hypoglycemic, hypothyroid, (the first to say 'hypochondriac' doesn't win). To put under, friction, squared, loss of function. the hype of milestones, a stone's throw (but my muscles are too weak to throw). Pain is a pedigree, landed, marked, signed, posted. Pot of goals, boiled dry, (What do you want to be when you grow up? I can't imagine myself grown up).

It's not dinner time yet, but there's nothing else to do. What do you want for dinner, my mother asks. I'm sitting at the table, closed, refrigerated. We'll have chicken, she says. The chicken has been defrosting for hours in the sink. She takes out baby carrots and baby leeks. I always wanted more babies, at least one more, but I couldn't because of your father. He never gave me any support with you and your sister. I had to do everything, he worked such long hours, he always went away for the weekend, he always did exactly what he wanted to do, oh, what's changed. I don't say anything. She cuts the chicken into smaller pieces. She says, You're the only one I can talk to, the only one who will actually listen to me. Not chicken again, I think. I feel as though we had chicken yesterday and the day before, and the day before that, and the day before that.

Beak, front, tip, edge, ease, pry. To sniff instead of to cry. To any question she says, 'I don't know.' Dragging a sigh, Can you pass me a tissue (No I'm not sad, she says in a sad voice). Linear bother hauling in, wallpaper expression, tearing away, tore it up. (No, I'm not crying, I don't have a cold, I just need a tissue.) There but. Not ever directly. Can you pass me a tissue, Therefore, (never really pouring out, never really resting).

At two o'clock I'm broccoli, at six o'clock I'm chicken, at eleven o'clock I'm potato. My father wants to warm the plates. My mother doesn't want to warm the plates. Cold plate, cold food, he says. My mother says, I just want to eat this food, I've spent too long making it. He warms his own plate. He warms my sister's plate, even though she's going to be late for dinner. Marguerite, my father says. I don't answer because I think he's talking to my mother and my mother doesn't answer because she thinks he's talking to me. Can you pass the salt. I pass him the salt. You shouldn't be having salt when you have high blood pressure, my mother says. My father looks at her. He dumps the whole salt shaker onto his plate. My wrist is sore, I can barely grip the fork. This has been going on for so long that I can't remember when it started, I say to the chicken. The chicken says, Tell me about it. My platelet count is high, I say to no one in particular.

I was speaking about myself, Although, because, whereas, provided that. To dibble: (How long have you had this). To daisy: (Is there a family history). Nominate a character (Who chose your name, Did your parents want a boy or a girl) (No, I never buy flowers because they're just going to die). That, which, who, whoever. Improper fraction. (Who chose your name.)

Often I find myself in the living room, looking at the blank TV as though I am watching a movie, with my knitting needles in my lap, until I become what I see, until I become a movie. I feel that my limbs have been stuck onto my body by a clumsy child.

Often my father comes into the living room holding a tube of glue, and asks if I have anything that needs gluing. I always say that I don't have anything that needs gluing. A disadvantage of most adhesives is that they do not form an instant bond, unlike many other joining processes, because the adhesive needs time to cure. Once my father pointed at my slipper. Look, the sole is starting to come off, maybe it needs gluing. No, it's fine, I said. He looked very disappointed.

in the shopping mall, not falling together, no, but my tote of symptoms, my Systemic. (I need to sit down.) Four receipts later: (That must be terrible, I have a similar sort of thing). i.e. Sympathy pathway (asymptotic), arbitrarily close without actually becoming the. Poured system. (requires an effort of reason.) (But that isn't a similar sort of thing. At all.) Poor system, your, swollen with, (I can't relate, Meanwhile, do you think I should buy this asymmetrical dress).

I find myself at a party, though I don't 'find myself' at the party, how did I get here, B took me to the party. There aren't any balloons, it's not that sort of party. There is alcohol but I don't touch it, I'm the only one not touching the alcohol. Why aren't you drinking? Many reasons, the first one is because I want people to ask me why I'm not drinking, the second one is because I'm on medication. B says more than once, I can't believe you're still here, if I wasn't drinking I wouldn't be here. Everywhere and in all things I have learnt both to be full and to be hungry. There are no nibbles at this party. I am disappointed. I don't really speak to anyone. There is a conversation about a film I have just seen, but I don't join in. I try to think of some topics for conversation but all that pops into my mind is *10 clues you may be in an emotionally abusive relationship* and *10 stars who died during the filming of a movie*. Someone asks me about myself. I say, My name is _______, I'm from _______, I went to university at _______, I've just written a novel called _______. And the someone says, Sorry, what? Your name is blank? You're from blank?

‘No’ lacks a bloodstream, she forgets it can be a complete sentence. A part and apart. Come to dinner, we’re having the skulls of mushrooms. (But there’s no room for me.) Socialise, generalise, compromise, improvise, circumcise, no surely not. Appetiser: what do you do, I mean for a living, no, what do you really do. (But I don’t take up any room.) My blood is too loud, I can’t think. (Dinner parties are not parties. Parties are not parties either.) She takes the long way home. (I’m sorry, I can’t come to dinner tonight, I’m going to get a headache.)

I am supposed to be looking out for side effects. The problem is that many of the side effects are the same as the symptoms I already experience. I lie on my bed. My heart seems to be beating faster, but maybe that is nothing new. Rain is coming through the window, but that's because the window is open. But what if my heart is actually beating faster than it is supposed to, what if this is a side effect. Now my heart is beating faster because I'm worried about my heart beating faster. My mother says she has wasted the last fifteen years of her life. What she means is that she has spent fifteen years with my father, which was fourteen years too long. Staying together for that long was a side effect of having children. In fact, their whole relationship was a side effect of a missed appointment and a broken window.

(shelf life) she was in the supermarket, hiding among the vegetables (corn, courgettes), shrink-wrapped, muddled, misprint, wheeled. Excuse me, you don't know me, but, are you the daughter of _______? Pushing a trolley into a stack of cans. Recital: (You look just like her). Rapped, hammerlock, verruca, batter. (Battered fish is on special). Recital: (Yes I am).

Take a position. Noon, we're in the kitchen again, I'm hungry. My mother takes a bite of her sandwich, Do you want this? You can have it if you want, I can make myself another. She is hungry. I feel hungry, I think, but I don't feel hunger, I feel that I think I'm hungry because I want to be hungry, because I haven't been hungry for months, it's a symptom. A bite of nothing. No, I'm fine, I can't decide what I feel like, I say. What is inside her sandwich? I'm having trouble imagining what is inside her sandwich. My position is the middle, not yes, the filling, I don't know, the filling is not always filling, not no. Do you even know who she is?

Indented, deep, pent, pent up. (I'd really like to go to ____, but the climate won't be good for my _____.) In the end, in the dent, in the pendant, I intended to do that thing but I didn't, If it weren't for my ______, I would. Indebted pet (Who looked after you? She was very good at looking after me).

The oily film of the weekend that covers the whole living room. The half-made soup, the lack of bread, the breadwinner. The illusion that motion is occurring. My half-made mother comes into the room, glances at me, opens the curtains. It was the biggest mistake of my life, she says. I try to pull the curtains shut from where I'm sitting. My mother pulls them open again. And for the record, she says, I hate that plant in here and I hate that plant in the bedroom. Why haven't they died yet? I never water them. The window is like a poster, I don't want to see it, I reach out to pull the curtain. Your father is having an affair, she says. I look at the floor. Can you believe it? she says. No, I say, I can't. But I'm lying, I can believe it, because it's happened, because I've been waiting for this to happen, because it's like a movie, it's just like a movie.

The song I'm listening to tells me that people take pictures of each other to prove that they loved one another, and to prove that they really existed. I don't listen to music very often, I don't like noise, it overwhelms my nervous system, my alpha brain waves are low.

I find a camera in a junk shop with film in it. I get the film developed that afternoon. There's a lot of damage, and many of these are underexposed, the woman says. Who's the baby in the photos? I think about some of the places I used to go. I used to go to the park and feed the ducks, and the bread would always run out halfway around the lake. I used to go to the beach and poke the sea anemones at low tide. I have to force myself to believe in those places, and to believe in myself in those places. I feel that I've stolen those memories from a passage in a novel. Oh, I say, that's my son.

It's not bedtime yet but there's nothing else to do. The dinner has been made, the dishes done, the television program viewed. Let's get ready for bed now, my mother says. The thickest sheet is still thinner than the lightest blanket, I say. I'm pretending to read a book. Come on, please, I don't want to be disturbed later. I look at my watch, but I'm not wearing a watch. However, I know it's early. I go to the bedroom and get into the bed without undressing.

My mother wants my father to leave for various reasons, and my father doesn't want to leave, for various reasons, some of which may be the same reasons. I could draw a Venn diagram. So my father has left but he has not left. I pull the blanket over me, the blanket that is intended to keep me warm. I haven't slept in my own bed for three months. My father is sleeping there. My mother told him that I need to sleep in her bed because I need looking after. Whenever a guest is coming round, I quickly go into my room and hide the evidence: my father's socks and shoes, his model railway magazines, his briefcase, etc. Then I unmake my bed and throw some of my books and dresses on it.

This arrangement was only supposed to last for a few weeks. My mother fills in a few squares of her crossword, then turns out the light, even if I'm still writing. I've started to work on an autobiography, I write a few lines each night. My mother always steals the blankets onto her side of the bed so most nights I wake up shivering. If I can't sleep, I lie there. If she can't sleep, she says, do you want to play Who Am I? That game where you think of a person and the other player has to figure out their identity by asking yes or no questions. I never want to play but I always do. Are you female? Are you alive? Are you in a current movie?

I was born at three o'clock in the morning on the 27th of October,

The doctor told my mother that she[1] couldn't have children, but a year later she was pregnant:

I spent a lot of time at the sick bay at school, waiting for my mother to arrive,

My mother had bought the house herself, before

It was difficult to find a comfortable position because everything[2] was painful;

My head felt incredibly foggy, as though

Instead of going out with friends, I[3] stayed at home with my mother,

After that, I decided not to speak[4] unless someone spoke to me first;[5]

1. Today, beyond the windows, there's a forest.
2. Pain needs room.
3. Watching the forest, waiting, weeping.
4. The conversation goes on.
5. Someone says, "Marguerite, Marguerite dear."

That year, I skipped school a lot,

She became panicked and fainted during the play – her heart was beating very fast and she felt like she couldn't breathe,

I never believed I was going to end up in a wheelchair,[6]

My[7] mother and sister were always

And because of the pain[8] and swelling in my wrist, I[9] couldn't write or

People would ask her what the matter was, and she would say, Nothing, this is just my face

6. I go slowly so as to gain time.
7. She seemed to have retreated back into her childhood.
8. A clump of nettles in flower.
9. If the story were acted in the theatre, it would be like this: Blackout in the auditorium. The play begins.

Before she had children, she bred Persian cats – she said that once she had children she didn't need the cats anymore,

I was the only one who didn't yell,

Her mother[10] used to say, I don't know what I'd do without you

I felt very far away, as though[11]

She spent hours trying to comb the knots out of her daughter's hair,

At first, it seemed like a novel experience,[12] but a week later I started to

My grandmother would say, We can't go out today,[13] it's raining

10. 'You're right, this is not normal weather for this time of year.'
11. The stranger speaks; it's not a question.
12. It's like paper or cottonwool.
13. Brown jacket splitting at the armholes and buttons missing.

She wasn't married to him, but she circled 'Mrs' when filling in forms,

I didn't want people to see me eating, so sometimes I ate my lunch in a toilet cubicle,[14]

My mother kept saying, You're going to fail[15] if

Each time my father's mother became pregnant she hoped for a girl;

I shared a room with my sister until I was thirteen

She watched her daughters closely at the park, but didn't play with them

My friends wouldn't let me borrow their notes for the classes I'd missed –

People my age should be at the height of their careers, my mother said,[16]

14. But when you think about it, you suddenly ask yourself who else did that.
15. But the deafness is relative.
16. Doors closing with a musical sound.

When I asked about the cause, the doctor[17] [18] said, If I knew that, I'd have a Nobel Prize –

At high school I was bullied by

She was taken away in an ambulance –

We went to the lake house every Christmas before it burnt down,

There was never enough food to eat[19] when my father[20] was young,

Or I chopped vegetables, set the table, folded laundry,

It was obvious that they thought she had fainted because of the nudity in the play,

17. Ask questions and don't wait for the answers.
18. Through a fog I see him laugh.
19. What makes me grow a bit thinner every day is shame.
20. Was he sad?

They all went swimming, but I wasn't able to because of[21]

At the hospital they said there was nothing wrong with her, they said it was 'all in her mind' –

On the way home from the farm I sat in the back seat and ate so many strawberries that my mother had barely enough to make jam

My father kept telling me that I should learn how to

When we were eight, my friend and I planned to run away from home;

I pretended[22] to be a vegetarian so that we would have something in common,

She[23] wore the bandage for a long time after the wound was healed, so that people would ask what was wrong

21. Whenever, between the silences, the text is read out, the actors should hang on every word, frozen, scarcely breathing, as if, in gradual stages, there was always more and more meaning to be extracted from the simplicity of the words.
22. All these efforts are designed to ward off silence.
23. Unhappiness had become a habit.

My father didn't have an affair, but it was easier to say that he did,[24]

She could have gone back to work straight away after having children but she[25] didn't want to do that,

You're not beautiful like your sister, my[26] mother would say,

My father was the youngest of four boys,

On the way home from the hospital I counted every bird that I[27]

I felt uncomfortable receiving pocket money – it was only a couple of dollars but sometimes I didn't take it,

She could count the number of her friends on one hand,

I didn't want to have to talk to anyone,

24. No part of the text should be delivered with any special emotion. No gestures either.
25. Fear comes and goes. Now it's back again.
26. Had looked like a flower; now she looked like a tree trunk.
27. For a long time she's somewhere else, alone.

And when the baby was born she named it after herself,[28]

I spent the afternoon looking at old photos and crying,[29]

When she was nine, she accidentally killed her brother's guinea pig

She'd never let me do my homework myself – she always wanted to do it for me

At that point, I had lived in the same house my whole life,

I won several prizes at the end of the year, and I asked if I could have some tadpoles as a reward,

The doctor prodded my stomach and asked, Does it hurt there – but he couldn't find anything wrong with me

28. But at this unsafe hour she was afraid to cross the street again.

29. The time between things, between people, the sort that other people throw away as of no importance to them.

Once he asked her if she wanted to get married and she said, Absolutely not

My[30] mother said, People your age should be at the height of good health

The doctor said, The immune system fails to recognise itself and starts attacking its own cells and tissues

She hated cooking dinner for the family each night,

Then I was able to be exempt from physical education and I was glad,

One day at kindergarten I got into an argument with a boy who claimed that my painting was his own, and my mother told me to be 'the bigger person' and let it go

She didn't have any hobbies,

I hadn't been able to run for seven years,[31]

30. The smell of imprisoned flowers.
31. She seems to be sleeping, says the actor.

During that time, I filled in so many forms – at the beginning I gave my title as 'Miss' but later on I began to circle 'Ms';

When she started to get labour pains, he told her to stop 'panicking'[32]

When I was home by myself, I searched for my sister's diary –

I couldn't concentrate on my work because it all just seemed so unreal[33] to me,

Only one of the tadpoles became a frog, but as a frog it hardly ate anything, and I spent hours hunched over the tank trying to make it eat,

I said I was just trying to eat healthily, but actually I was[34] trying to be thin –

She didn't keep a diary because she didn't want anyone to read[35] it,

32. Very early in my life it was too late.
33. Still this room I write to you from.
34. This evening I think about myself.
35. The reading of the book will act as theatre for the story.

If I got a good grade, she'd say, That's because I helped you,

I filled in the form and added up my score, I got a point for having symptoms lasting more than six weeks,[36] I almost felt like I was winning something,[37]

Or she would say, But it's my house:

My mother said she hated it, so I never wore it, I put it in a plastic bag in the bottom drawer,

After that I stopped having birthday parties, because I didn't have any friends to invite,[38]

You're just like your father, my mother would say to my sister,

36. But today a much more terrible ripening was taking place.
37. Her light tone has in it a certain amount of courage and the secret wish that the doctor would not contradict her.
38. Cheap melodrama.

I kept telling my mother that she should separate[39] from my father,

Once, a group of boys threw my coat and books over the fence at the

I looked at my parents as though I had never seen them before –

When she was thirteen, she had to have an operation to remove a large mole from her back,

My favourite stuffed animal was a grey rabbit, until one day my mother commented that the rabbit had been given to me by that 'awful' female 'friend' of my father's,

I was always trying to placate[40] my sister and

I looked at my body[41] as if it didn't belong to me,

39. Answer: Not yet, but it will come.
40. So I'm on my own.
41. I wake up, so I know I've been asleep.

My mother wouldn't allow us to cut our hair until

The sofa had a huge hole in it and she needed to buy a new one, but she couldn't find the 'perfect' sofa so she didn't buy anything –

I didn't want to go to school and I didn't want to stay at home,

She had long black hair and blue eyes,[42]

My mother said, I can't separate from him right now because the doctor says his blood pressure is very high

If I hadn't been sick, then I[43] could have

She spent an evening looking at all my father's photos and listening to all his stories, but when it was time to present her photos, he said he was too tired and went to bed

42. I'm still looking at the photographs.
43. The story of my life doesn't exist. Does not exist.

Whenever the subject of marriage came up, I said, I'm never going to get married[44] –

I dropped my mother's special bracelet in the toilet; maybe it fell in while I was flushing or maybe I flushed after it fell in,

My mother and sister were always[45] arguing, but they never spent any time together,

Once, I hid her glasses and everyone looked for them for hours – I pretended to look –

On the way to the hospital I kept thinking, I can't believe this is happening again[46]

But I didn't ask her to do it for me, I just wanted help and

I felt so tired, like I[47] couldn't be bothered to breathe,

I couldn't remember the last time I had hugged or been hugged by anyone,

44. It doesn't exist in detail, only principle.
45. It happened every day.
46. The first line of any book that is already written.
47. Threadbare.

My mother and I sat in the waiting[48] room,

She moved house a lot during her childhood,

The next day there was a vase of flowers in my bedroom – my mother never usually bought flowers because they died so quickly –

She went to the library and got forty books on the subject,

She always helped her mother with the chores, while her brothers played games and

I'd wake up from a nightmare and couldn't go back to sleep,[49]

But I was glad that I didn't have to go to school for a while,

I[50] started to cry because she was crying,

As we pulled up outside our house my mother said, Don't tell your father what the doctor said about

48. She felt like a swimmer about to dive.
49. The auditorium is blacked out, says the actor. The play keeps beginning again, with every sentence, every word.
50. A broken window.

I sat in my room[51] playing the same song over and over,

Apparently, a few weeks after my sister was born, I asked if we could take her back to the hospital,

She managed to get casual work at her daughters' primary school, and then their intermediate school, and then their high school –

That summer I tried to write an autobiography but I had trouble finishing my[52]

But after she followed her boyfriend to London, it became quite clear that he didn't want to continue the relationship,

My sister was always asking our parents for money, but I hardly ever asked for anything,

So I spent hours hiding behind my bedroom door in the dark,[53]

51. Chance is surrounded by a floating odour of children's rooms.
52. I am not hungry: tonight I am unable to digest my life.
53. The words aren't there, nor the sentence to put the words into.

My sister went to her bedroom when I[54] came into the living room,

I wore long shapeless dresses, I avoided eating in public, and I wore sunglasses all the time, even when it wasn't sunny,

If she hadn't had children, then she could[55] have

At the time, no one told her that the mole was cancerous[56] –

They told my sister she needed to get a job and my sister said, But Marguerite doesn't have a job,

Once, during P.E. at high school, I overheard two boys discussing who they thought were the ugliest people in the class, and my name was mentioned –

She made sure she was always available to pick them up from school,

54. 'You're sad – I can't bear it when you're sad.'
55. There are some people who are not waiting for anything.
56. I still have so many things to tell you.

I ran out of the classroom crying[57] and

When my father left he took various kitchen utensils, including the sieve, so we had to eat food with a little added water,

She had to help her get dressed because[58]

Her father ran over the family cat,[59]

My mother drove me to and from school so I didn't aggravate my legs by walking up and down the hill,

I didn't let myself fall asleep until I heard my mother go to bed,

My sister eventually had her hair cut, but I kept[60] my hair long –

57. 'It's nothing, just emotion.'
58. The pain is so great it can't breathe.
59. She did not ask her sister any questions, because her face told everything.
60. It was built on the past.

Then I stopped sleeping over at friends' houses because I was afraid[61] that my family would die

She did not feel comfortable leaving the house without wearing make-up,

On the internet I read: Pay close attention to your doctor's directions – some people who mistakenly took drug X once daily instead of weekly experienced very severe reactions or died,

If we weren't at an appointment, we had[62] just been to one or were just about to go to one,

Once I stole an orange from a supermarket because I couldn't work out how to use the self-service machine, and I was too embarrassed to ask

She tried to cheer her up by buying her flowers and magazines,

On that holiday my sister broke her nose and I felt sick and tense for weeks afterwards, as though it was my nose that had been broken,

61. I suddenly remember something I've been told about fear.
62. For those who suffer, time does not exist.

Later that year, I became[63] increasingly

She was on the train when she suddenly felt that she was going to die, and she

My only visitor was a girl who I'd been best friends[64] with at primary school;

I didn't sit with everyone at the dinner table; I lurked in the kitchen, eating the watery soup from the flask I had brought with me,

I felt guilty[65] every time I saw someone wearing a bracelet,

I kept baking biscuits and cupcakes but didn't eat any of them

Every Friday afternoon when she was eight, she told her primary school teacher that she was moving to Canada in the weekend and so would not be at school on Monday

63. There's no sound left but the gusts of wind in the forest.
64. It's the beginning of forgetting.
65. The space for it existed in me.

That year, both of her parents were having affairs, and everyone in the family knew what was happening but no one said anything[66]

I became very thin, I wore cardigans in the middle of summer to hide my emaciated arms,

One night I sat in bed with a coin in my hand, thinking about swallowing the coin in order to become sick and get my parents' attention

She asked her mother for dating advice, but it was bad advice and she lost both of the boys she was dating,

She was so stressed[67] that she developed a bald spot;

Therefore I[68] stopped caring about birthdays and Easter and Christmas,

66. The actors need not necessarily be professionals. But they must always read the book out loud and clear, doing all they can to exclude any memory of ever having read it before, endeavouring to come to it every evening as if for the first time.
67. 'The sun is gone. It came and went, the way it does in a prison.'
68. I've grown older. I suddenly know it.

I had to change[69] schools because

I didn't want it to be my birthday, I wasn't ready,[70]

When she was first living in that house, she rang her mother when she came home at night, and checked every room for intruders while

I had just been given a new bicycle and now[71] my legs were too swollen to ride it,

My sister demanded pocket money from my father, but my mother didn't agree with

He was shouting and throwing papers on the ground, and then he went out the back door and slammed the door so hard that the glass panel in the door shattered,

She didn't think she could go back to work because[72] she had to care for

The frog eventually died of starvation, and in a way its death was a relief,

69. But now there is hope, and pain is implanted in hope.
70. Some coloured crayons and a child's drawing.
71. The room she entered was almost completely dark.
72. Certain memories, certain particular regrets.

So I had to stay in the car because I[73] could barely walk,

She told her that she was probably tired and that she would feel better in the morning

I overheard them talking about how concerned they were about my weight, and I smiled,

She made soup for the family on the weekend but complained about the

Every time I went to the beach I couldn't relax because I was thinking[74] about tidal waves –

But I didn't feel better in the morning, I felt worse,[75]

After about twenty minutes of shouting, my mother came into my room and asked if she could share my bed[76] and I said yes

73. You get used to it... You get used to not getting used to it.
74. You can't call this thinking.
75. I don't have any memories.
76. For five minutes the stage will remain frozen, full of people asleep.

When I was ten,[77] my parents went to Europe for three months, leaving my sister and me to stay with my uncle,

She wrote a letter to the school explaining my

I broke my mother's special piggybank and I cried so much that I was almost sick

By the time I changed[78] schools I wasn't wearing the neck brace anymore,

She was always ringing up the

When she became angry I said I was joking and that the bracelet was in my room somewhere

For example, every time I passed the bookshelf I felt guilty for all the books my mother had given me[79] that I hadn't read,

77. With a beginning and an end, unforgettable and yet you've forgotten it. I forget.
78. Pine trees wrenched from the ground by their roots.
79. Always off in the heart of the absolute pain of thought.

The doctor just said there was no cause and no[80] cure, and if I didn't take those drugs I would end up in a wheelchair[81]

I felt embarrassed when I had to buy food,

The first time I wore my mother's shoes, I broke my ankle

My sister wanted a ride to school but my mother said no, because there was nothing wrong with her and she needed the exercise

She felt sick so she didn't eat and then she felt sick from not eating,

Sometimes, at school, people would ask me[82] what was wrong and I would say, Nothing, this is just my face

80. The heat's oppressive, all the windows are wide open and there's not a breath of air.
81. The door shuts.
82. A woman with a sallow complexion, slim, not beautiful, but interesting.

Once, in the middle of a dinner party, she left the table and drove home because he wouldn't stop flirting with the host

My father had planned to take my sister and me to Europe at the end of the year and my sister said, I'm sorry but it seems unfair if we have to cancel just because you can't travel,

At my uncle's house we[83] weren't allowed to have friends over

My mother was too sick[84] to stay and had to come back to New Zealand,

For my[85] birthday my mother bought me a canary cage – she said, when you're better, I'll buy you a canary

83. In the night the void of absence is vast.
84. The room is empty. The only furniture is two chairs and a table.
85. She puts the black silk over her face. She says, 'I'm a writer.'

I stopped reading and writing for a year afterwards,[86]

My mother made us go on a long hike in terrible weather

She struggled[87] to cope with

I was so angry with her that I tried to make myself faint, in protest

My sister and I were sitting in our room listening to them shouting, we knew that we couldn't leave our room for a while – I was eating an apple and thought, I should have more snacks in my room for situations like these

But she still felt like she didn't know what she wanted to do in her life:[88]

86. It's dark. I can't see the words I've written anymore.
87. Like a swimmer caught between a mudbank and a rock.
88. 'Are you afraid? Afraid of yourself?'

She didn't try to pretend to like the presents we gave her;[89]

I glanced in the mirror and became frightened[90] because I didn't recognise myself[91]

Her 21st birthday was spent with family, and her mother made a cake which didn't have enough sugar in it,

At the supermarket I hit my ankle hard on the side of the trolley, and then three days later my ankle and knee swelled up painfully[92]

And her mother had had panic attacks while pregnant with her,

While they were away, the bullying got worse but

She said that my father didn't drive her to hospital straight away because he was writing a fax and making sandwiches and a thermos of tea,

89. It's a matter of indifference to me; I don't even think about it being a matter of indifference.
90. It's rather dark, divided into two sections both the same size.
91. 'I'm right in front of you and you don't see me –'
92. At last she can weep without being asked why.

All the dresses and jumpers in my wardrobe had once been my mother's:

I had to go to the hospital because another student hurt me,

She started keeping a notebook[93] about her daughter –

Once, a therapist asked me if I had ever been abused and I laughed and said, No, not unless I have repressed the memory,

I only ever saw my parents hug and kiss each other once, when I was six[94]

She hoped the holiday[95] would cheer her up, but it seemed to have the opposite effect

I showed a short story to a friend and she sighed and asked if my mother had read it – I said she had, and that the story wasn't 'true', but some of the feelings were;[96]

93. It's more necessary than you think.
94. That period of her life became so embellished in memory that, looking back, it seemed almost a time of happiness.
95. The sunrise, the empty sea.
96. Their expression is one of fear, distress, guilt at having been the centre of attention, both for the actors on the stage and for the audience.

I went into my mother's room and she was sitting in bed crying and my uncle was sitting at the end of the bed,[97]

She spent all her spare time on the internet, searching for answers

My father arrived halfway through the prize-giving ceremony,

All of her friends were at the height of their careers and making a lot of money:

My sister asked me what was wrong – I told her I was in a lot of pain[98] and didn't feel well, and she said, I don't know what to say,

I refused to go to the school ball in the last year of high school,

I wanted to live in a different city[99]

97. Skirted around all these things without really tackling them.
98. Is such that it can't be described.
99. Every street has its memories, its shrieks, its shouts, its sobs.

Years later, my sister said: I didn't know it was like that, that it was that bad – why didn't I know about[100]

The doctor said it would help but it didn't,

She liked working and

The therapist I was seeing was the same woman my mother had seen fifteen years earlier, and she was also friends with my grandmother,

Every time she tried to discuss something that bothered her, he told her to stop being 'negative' and to stop dwelling on the past[101] –

We spent hours[102] in a small room while the nurse and physiotherapist took casts of my legs and wrist so they could

She always said, Choose better than I did: don't marry someone like[103] your father –

100. Like everything else, they happen to you. Afterward, they have happened to you. They might happen to anyone.
101. Six months? An hour? A second?
102. In recollection it's like the sound-track of a film turned up to high, deafening.
103. The comparison is senseless.

When they came home, I had done half the dishes and my mother told me to sit down, and instructed my sister to finish them,

She felt that people just 'walked all over' her,

Before I started at a new primary school, my mother attempted to homeschool[104] me:

She thought that once he left, her daughter's health would improve,[105]

She spent[106] thousands of dollars on

Her mother never cooked enough food – she'd make two servings and divide it between four

My mother said, I have just realised[107] that when your sister asks me what I am doing tomorrow, it means that she wants to spend time with me

104. You don't remember, it creates no memory.
105. I try to reduce the situation to its lowest terms.
106. Like water from a vase's too-narrow neck.
107. A thin ray of moonlight.

I decided that I wanted to go to university in a different city[108]

I went home with him, and after he kissed me I felt compelled to tell him what was wrong[109] with me,

She resented the fact that he went away in the weekends without

My sister said she couldn't get a job because of her stomachaches and headaches,

Then we talked on the phone[110] – my mother said, Are you okay, you sound okay but I'm not sure if you are okay, you don't have to pretend with me,

108. 'How long have you been planning this?'
109. Kept from despair by a thin layer of make-up.
110. I just wanted to hear your voice.

At the time, I didn't mention it once in my diary[111] or

My mother's unsolicited advice was simply, Sex is not like having a cup of tea

If you complained about being bullied, the teachers would say, Did you tell them 'Stop it, I don't like it,'

My father subscribed to a model railway magazine called *Back Track*;

In my notebook I wrote down the names and numbers of local hairdressers,

She was grateful when her therapist got cancer, because it meant that she didn't have to see her anymore and she didn't have to tell her that she didn't want to see her anymore

111. 'No one can know what's happening in this room. And no one can say what's going to happen, either.'

But at the time, I had no one I could talk to,

Most nights I was going to bed[112] at 3 a.m.,

She told her to hide the blood test results from her father,

On the phone, she said, you're not heading for a nervous breakdown I hope – I was your age when I[113] had my first breakdown[114]

Her flatmates turned against her

My father said that we didn't do anything together anymore, and suggested we go kayaking – when I told him I couldn't go kayaking, he seemed bewildered

She always said yes when people asked favours of her and then[115] [116]

My mother said, I don't know what I'd do without you,[117]

112. She switches on the lights. And lies herself down in the middle of the light, where she has dragged the sheets.
113. Now the facts lie buried under forty years.
114. One can only raise happiness on a foundation of despair. I think I will be able to start building.
115. 'I'm tired, as if I were dying.'
116. She had allowed them to rest all the burdens of their lives on her for so long that she had become like a servant who suffered for them.
117. The stranger doesn't answer.

I couldn't walk up the stairs, so

She felt that she had wasted the last fifteen years of her life[118] –

But she had two young children to think about,

My sister was screaming and crying because our mother hadn't bought her any birthday presents yet

Then we heard him get in the car and drive away – He'll be back, my grandmother said, but he didn't come back – he drove all the way back home, leaving us without a car in the

But she didn't feel she could do that because her daughter was unwell,[119]

Then I started reading[120] again –

118. It would make a good film.
119. The tide is a long way out.
120. When one is cold, one should try to get warm.

I kept thinking[121] about the future[122] –

But I could never say[123] what I[124]

And my shoes and coat were not waterproof; I started walking through deep puddles on purpose,

I was writing again,[125]

And she said to me, I will never be happy until you are well,[126]

121. She had forgotten that she wanted to die.
122. I'm going to write. That's what I see beyond the present moment.
123. 'I don't say anything. I never tell the truth.'
124. 'Don't go off on a tangent to make me forget what I was thinking of…'
125. When things go wrong, there is now someone in me who says yes.
126. Music will be heard, classical music, recognisable because it has been heard before the play, and before that again, in life.

I ask the inside and no other side. What passes me by. I can't walk today. I make a telephone from this information and call you up. 'My mother or father needed me to be happy.' No answer. For children who have difficulty bending, a long-handled reacher and sock-aid is recommended. It is like this, or it is like that. Who am I comparing for. The doll doesn't have any hair. Sometimes it is better to have no expectations. In most the disease is progressive for life. For the time being I let the things in my hand fall to the ground.

She is fourteen years old, still young. The first task of the immune system is distinguishing self from non-self. Why do you think your suffering is important. She is twenty-one years old, still old. What do you think of me. I am here again. I am back here and further from it. What argument can be used now. Inside my pulse I am making lanterns.

Does one write 'Illness is a state of mind', or 'I believe illness is a state of mind'. A wheel, together with an axle, overcomes fiction. Responsibility is not the same as blame. I don't think I make a good first impression. Show me how to look forward to things.

Everything is a painting if you look long enough. Symptoms are often non-specific initially. Was it March or April. When do these things actually begin. 'I will plait your hair before you go to bed, so that it doesn't strangle you while you sleep.' People are learning to be people by talking and crying. I see birds in the grass without birds.

A pattern with secondary branches. 'I know it's worse for you, but this places a lot of burden on me.'

The symptoms are no longer merely uncomfortable because they're unpleasant; they are now uncomfortable because of what you believe they mean about how your life will be from this point on.

Many of us do not deserve our epithets. For each year that passes, I get a little more used to it, or I get used to not getting used to it. My grandmother said, 'I read your poems, I understood them, I'm not sure if I should tell you that, I know you like to be obscure.' If I write about it long enough, will it go away. Sympathy is an asymptote. I was scared to be independent. But I could change my name if I wanted to. I could change my name to Zarah, for example.

Trying to think of some way out. I can be sad for any number of reasons but none is enough. As the pathology progresses, the inflammatory activity leads to erosion and destruction of the joint surface. Give it meaning and move on. What meaning. I have made the same birthday wish for the last seven years. Now, instead of saying 'goodbye', I say 'take care'.

Photographs sell milk until midnight. Perhaps I will be here for years and years and there will be no story. I wrote, 'I am afraid of the things I desire the most' and he wrote, 'But you are not writing about desire.' I desire to be well, but first I have to imagine it. What thing isn't about desire.

I pray without realising I'm praying. I am up on the main path now; the lights from the houses are clearer. Should I write 'the illness' or 'my illness'. If I have this for the rest of my life, is this my purpose in life. What can replace this. Sometimes I walk backwards. Would you prefer good things happened, or interesting things. Pain goes on and then goes. Every move I make seems bigger than it really is.

But everyone is just trying to feel less lonely. I need to hold the handrails on both sides. I cannot tell you what to do, because I do not know. How whole is your 'whole life'. I haven't said everything I wanted to say. I dreamt I could run again.

‘Thank your illness for looking after you so well.’ Just because we don’t know the reason doesn’t mean there isn’t one. When a new yeast cell breaks away, it leaves a round scar on its parent. We are not ill, but needy. Everything I’ve done so far I’ve done to care for myself. The happening is still happening. ‘Ultimately I think this is important, the right thing.’ So do I.

Notes

The footnotes on pages 36–72 were sourced from the following books:

Duras, Marguerite. *Blue Eyes, Black Hair* (Pantheon Books, 1987).
Duras, Marguerite. *La Douleur* (Éditions P.O.L, 1985).
Duras, Marguerite. *The Lover* (Pantheon Books, 1985).
Yourcenar, Marguerite. *A Coin in Nine Hands* (Farrar, Straus and Giroux, 1982).
Yourcenar, Marguerite; Katz, Dori, (ed). *Fires* (Farrar, Straus and Giroux, 1981).

This edition of the text is mostly identical to the 2014 edition (Hue & Cry Press) apart from minor formatting changes, and edits made on pages 17, 19, 23, 29, 31 and 85.

About the Author

Zarah Butcher-McGunnigle is a writer and counsellor from Auckland, currently living in Melbourne. She is the author of *Nostalgia Has Ruined My Life* and *Leaves Fall Off to Create Drama*.